FATHERLESS YET FABULOUS

A REFLECTION TO A BETTER YOU

Tierra C. L. Oliver

ISBN 978-1-0980-3933-2 (paperback)
ISBN 978-1-0980-3934-9 (digital)

Christian Faith Publishing
832 Park Avenue
Meadville, PA 16335
www.christianfaithpublishing.com

All images designed by freepik

Printed in the United States of America

AFFIRMATIONS

With pain, there often comes purpose. With each trial, there is a triumph! At the tender age of seventeen, I lost my father. My father was a strong man, a big man with a broad chest, size 15 triple-E shoe (yes, one shoe. He lost his left leg when he was three) and large hands. He had a beautiful voice; when he would sing, it was like an instrument was in his vocal cords. He studied and was superbly intelligent. He was my hero, but my hero was also a man who struggled with an evil spirit, a spirit of sexual addiction. This spirit tore apart my family when I was ten. It was the first time I saw my hero for something less than divine. He let the spirit of sexual perversion serve as a hiding place for deeply seeded issues. He was boggled by pain and insecurity, and this addiction plagued him from the time he was crudely exposed to sexuality during his childhood. He struggled with many uncertainties, leading him to a path of selling drugs, toting guns and drug and alcohol abuse. I was a gift to him that he never thought he'd have, but underneath his durable shell lived a broken boy. And when I was seventeen, it was all over. It was gone just like that. I was in pain due to his death but was left questioning who my father was. I was devastated. I searched. Looking for something to replace this crater in my heart.

After several failed relationships, I was left with a broken heart. I felt lost and far away from God. During these dark years, I often felt as if I was walking in a trance. Then I had my daughter who breathed life into me. Unexpectedly I had become a single mother. What? Me? Eventually, I began to forgive myself and accept that I loved my hero despite his faults. Due to my story, *Fatherless Yet Fabulous* was created. I am a person who has overcome hardships, and I felt as if it was my responsibility to help hurting youth. Lord breathe life into FYF. May its work reach whoever is in need! You may be fatherless, but you are oh so fabulous!

Love is patient. Love is kind. Love listens and does not harm. Love makes you feel like you can fly. Love is the act of giving your true self. Someone loves you more than you know.

Today I affirm that I am enough. I am made in the image of God; therefore, I am a reflection of perfection. I affirm that I am worth it, and I will love myself in this worth.

Your true self is not a cliché; that self is the bare bones of you. The girl behind the bags, shoes, social media, sex, money, and game.
Your true self is all you have to give; It is the best part of who you are.

Why didn't he love me?
—*says the little girl
inside of you*

Today I affirm that I am more than a conqueror through Christ. Although I am living in this world, I am not of this world. I affirm that the unique gifts within me *will* be used because I will not rest until I share them with the world!

If he only knew how much
I need him, love him.
I waited and waited for the day
that would turn from, "I'm gonna
come get you" *to* "I'm outside."

Today I affirm that my past life and
mistakes do not define me. Even the
times I have hurt others, I forgive
myself. I affirm that I am divinely
created; my heart is good. I will
expect and only accept positivity
and love from myself and others.

You think no one sees you, but they
do. They see your beauty, they
see your strength, they see your
smile, your light, your worth.
They see you!

Today I affirm that inner peace
comes from having the courage to
do what genuinely makes you happy
despite the risk...just go for it!

Why did he hurt me?
Didn't he hear me scream, "Stop!"

Today I affirm that the decisions and
pain from my past will be buried along
with regret. I am free! I pray that passion
will powerfully push my current actions.
I promise myself that today and every
future day will be filled with joy!

The worth of you is still very bountiful.
The truth of who you are is beneath
the hurt, it's beneath the late-night
touches in your "no-no square." The
fact of who you are in the purest part
of you, the calm before the storm.

Why didn't *he love me enough* to be there?

Today I affirm that I cannot change time. If I could, I would press rewind and delete the painful experiences. That is not an option, but the beauty of creating purpose out of pain is now my conscious choice.

His choices do not define you,
his mistakes and his inability to
get past himself to reach the
joy that lives within you.
The pain is over your best part is here.

Today I affirm that love doesn't
just happen, it is a choice. I
choose to love myself, and this is
a choice I will make each day.

Why am I not *good enough?*

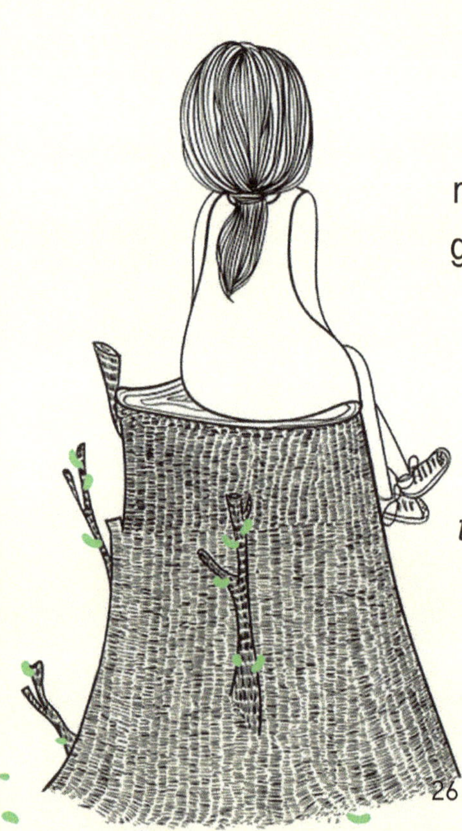

The best part of
you is not about his
faults. It's not about
the dad that he
couldn't be. It's not
about the games
he missed, the
birthdays that he
never called for, the
gifts that you hoped
he would buy.
*The best part of
you is the warrior
that climbed
through the hole he
left in your heart
toward the healing
you will capture!*

Chaos breeds anxiety, and anxiety
confuses the divine purpose
of the soul. Live free.

I don't understand who I am.
Why did *he violate my body?*

One day soon, the shame that he caused you will bring forth new life. The same body you grew to loathe because of what he did will be the *gateway to life for your children. In them, you will find a love like no other.*

Today I affirm that I will not live a life
of mediocrity. I affirm that the small
flame that burns within my spirit will
ignite into a life of successful passion.
My daily passion will be a reflection
of my life's purpose. I was not created
by happenstance, and I will live in
the excellence of divine conviction.

Life is a *canvas.*

On this canvas, you will paint the colors of your life. You can relate to all of the hues that will paint the picture of who you are and what a masterpiece you will create!

Today I affirm that although I feel
the pain of neglect and the burden
of singular parenthood. It does not
make me less of a mother. I was
given this special child because God
knew that I am the mother for her.
I will not question God's choice.

Feel safe to describe your darkest, loneliest time. Could you call him during this time? Now imagine rescuing yourself from that place, *what would you do first to change this place of loneliness?*

His death drained such life from
me that the emptiness which
remained was free to be filled by
any *man who professed love.*

Today I affirm that I will no longer abuse my mind or body. Every sensory reception that I allow into my personal space will be of growth, maturity, purpose, and will fortify the woman that I am becoming.

But one after the other, they
lied, manipulated, and left *my
barren heart broken.*

The anger and regret that
remains are all I have left.
I control just how angry I want
to be, and I am so *mad*!

Today I affirm that I will not apologize
for being great. I was created to
live a life of abundant overflow.

That anger has controlled you, has snatched your love, your peace, and your mind. The time has come to *give yourself permission to forgive and release.*

Permit yourself to *love crazy and unconditionally, then start with yourself!*

Tell yourself your beauty
is bold with an abundance
of gifts.
Then believe it!

Today I affirm that my beauty is more
than the way I look, the shape of my
body, or the type of clothes I wear. The
beauty within me has been cultivated.
Through turmoil, it has been refined
and defined. I am internally beautiful.

Move out of the mystery of
your pain and start to live in the
newness of a powerful you!

Start today! *Forgive, release, and restore.*
Put the pieces of *you together*!

Pray for understanding and
clarity, allow the power of peace
to strengthen your soul.
Now walk in the gift of grace.

Fear and faith don't mix.
Always choose faith.

He can't take your gift because
he didn't give you it.
*You are chosen and infinitely
loved by the Highest.*

You are beautiful. Life
demands your strength.
A new start is yours to take today.
The pain of your past is the
complexity of a fabulous future.
*Oh, my dear, you are
fatherless yet fabulous!*

Today I affirm that I deserve a life
of peace and happiness, that life is
mine, and I'm going to get it! And
never forget you may be fatherless,
but *you are* oh so *fabulous*!

ABOUT THE AUTHOR

Tierra C. L. Oliver is a board-certified family nurse practitioner and a single mother from Newburgh, New York. Newburgh has often been referred to as amongst the most dangerous in the New York State. However, when one looks beyond this, the root of the issue often comes back to fatherlessness and poverty. The two, in many ways, go hand in hand. Having experienced the grief of losing her father and later becoming a single mother, Ms. Oliver challenged herself. She challenged herself to take a very difficult time and use it to push her forward. Fatherless Yet Fabulous, LLC is a mentoring and life-coaching company created in 2016. In this twenty-one-day reflection, you will be challenged. Be honest with yourself and begin to move forward!

9 781098 039332